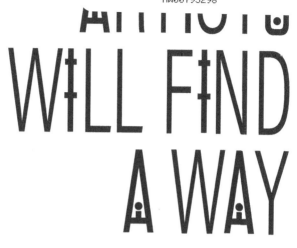

ARTISTS
WILL FIND
A WAY

A STUDIO NAVIGATION GUIDE

FRAN GARDNER

Synergy Publishing Group
Belmont, NC

Artists Will Find a Way: A Studio Navigation Guide
Fran Gardner

Published by Synergy Publishing Group, Belmont, NC

Cover and interior art by Fran Gardner
Layout and design by Melisa Graham

Softcover, April 2024, ISBN 978-1-960892-17-1
E-book, April 2024, ISBN 978-1-960892-18-8

CONTENTS

INTRODUCTION

With deep thanks to the University of South Carolina Lancaster, where I honed my teaching skills, I was awarded a sabbatical for the spring 2020 semester. My project was to further my book and to make new studio work for upcoming gallery and museum exhibitions. We all know what happened in spring 2020. Suddenly, and with little warning, our world changed dramatically, globally. One day I was in New York going to galleries, museums, and art fairs, drinking in all the city has to offer those of us who love art, and the next day, it all closed—indefinitely. Like dominoes, all of my upcoming exhibitions and projects were either canceled or postponed. Like so many other artists, I fell into a deep questioning of the purpose and value of art. What I discovered led me to this book.

Here is one thing I know: artists will find a way to make art; they always do. Even under the most dire and repressive of circumstances. And that art will speak to the culture and time from which it came. Artists during the pandemic found innovative and surprising ways to share their art. There is no question that art will continue; it always has. But how we view, learn, and teach art has changed post-pandemic. And many of these changes are wonderful. For example, check out the Metropolitan Museum of Art's series on Connections, a great way to learn about art through themes.[1] I integrated those into the online classes that I taught as a result of the pandemic, the first in my thirty-two-year teaching career, with great success.

Artists will find a way.

Through many years of working with college students, I developed skills in making, writing about, and teaching art. I suddenly realized that I had a book. I had created lectures, artist talks, essays, motivational exercises, theories, assignments, and methods. In short, I had concepts about art, theories that I hold true as an artist and teacher; definitions that develop those concepts so that one understands the methodology; and action plans or assignments to achieve them. I also had the encouragement of artist-friends who wanted me to write this book, who had unwavering confidence in me to do it and the absolute certainty that I would do it well. I thank these artists for trusting me with their creative development, sharing their vulnerabilities and their lives as artists with me.

Because of COVID-19, I realized that this book was a way for me to not only share but also assist, a way to offer artists proven methods that are often learned in group settings like classes or retreats. But through this book, these methods

---

1. "Connections," The Metropolitan Museum of Art, accessed March 18, 2024, https://www.metmuseum.org/connections.

can be available when we are alone in our own studios, as we so often are. One of the most satisfying experiences of so many artists is getting together—retreats, residencies, critiques, exhibitions ways to interact and learn from the art and one another. This book is the stuff of classes, retreats, coaching, and mentoring, but in your own studio. It is an immediate resource for when you stumble.

Now, in the post-pandemic world, we can go to retreats, residencies, and classes again. We can have exhibitions and group critiques. My goal for this book is for you, the artist, to use it to work independently in your studio, *and* use these concepts in group experiences, shared interactively in person or online.

While the book is written in a linear format, artists don't think or act that way. Feel free to peruse the chapters, find the issue most relevant to you, and start there. In other words, move around the book like you'd move around a canvas or a sculpture, working on the parts that you are drawn to, that you feel a need to address.

Art is a *discipline* with everything that word implies— methods, practice, development—but it is also a *creative* experience with all that word implies—intuition, innovation, and vision. The artist's job is to strike a balance between discipline and creativity so that the art and the artist can move through the provocative and expansive scope of creativity with confidence, assured that they have a voice and a message for the world.

CHAPTER 1:
YOUR ART'S PURPOSE

E very artist, at some point, questions their art's purpose. Why am I making all this art, even when sales are flat, even when I have a full inventory, even when I don't have a studio, even when, even when? Clearly, this drive to make art goes far beyond issues of sales and inventory. It goes beyond issues of space and finances. It sometimes seems to go beyond logic. So let's talk about purpose. Defining your art's purpose helps you to understand your art and why you make it, to understand your role as a cultural voice for your generation, to see avenues for shifting your voice and message (whether you seek a radical or a subtle shift), and to see places where your interests can speak to others through your work.

In Alain de Botton and John Armstrong's book *Art as Therapy*, the authors present a case for art as a pragmatic tool through which viewers can engage their world. They define a tool as "an extension of the body that allows a wish to be carried out, and that is required because of a drawback in our physical make-up. A knife is a response to our need, yet inability, to cut. A bottle is a response to our need, yet inability, to carry water."[2] They go on to present seven "functions" of art, taking away the mystery of how to look at, understand, and find art personally meaningful. They pose the question, "What if art has a purpose that can be defined and discussed in plain terms? Art can be a tool, and we need to focus more clearly on what kind of tool it is—and what good it can do for us."[3]

What if we shifted our thinking and considered art as a necessity, like a tool, essential to our existence? As useful in our daily lives as cars, airplanes, computers, and cell phones? If art is a useful, everyday tool, and if you are an artist, then what key purpose, what essential necessity does your art serve?

THE TOOLS

While de Botton and Armstrong's discussion is written primarily from the perspective of the art *viewer*, with a bit of a shift in perspective, it is also a wonderful resource for the art *maker*. I have taken their basic premise of the seven functions of art, added to those, and shifted the perspective to serve the needs of the art maker.[4]

---

2. Alain de Botton and John Armstrong, *Art as Therapy* (London: Phaidon Press Limited, 2013), 5.

3. de Botton and Armstrong, *Art as Therapy*, 4

4. de Botton and Armstrong, *Art as Therapy*, 58–9. There is a deeper explanation of each in "The Seven Functions of Art" on pages 8–56. With deep gratitude, I give the authors all of the credit for the concept of pragmatic tools for viewing art and acknowledge that I took liberties in suggesting the same idea from the artist's perspective.

Memory

Art can help us remember a given situation: who and what was there and what it looked like. But perhaps more acutely, art can help us remember what it *felt* like, the mood, emotion, and sensory experience of an event. In abstraction, this is often what the artist is conveying—the sensation of the person, place, or time. In this way, think about how art can enhance both our physical memories and our sensory memories.

Hope

Hope is a yearning and a desire, often coming from a place of darkness, but looking toward something better. It is a confidence or trust in the future to bring about positive change. A hopeful work of art doesn't remove worry, fear, and distress but suggests a deeper comfort and grace, even in the face of a troubling and demanding reality. Hope is a precarious position. It makes no promises, but shows us possibility.

Sorrow

Everyone experiences sorrow; we wouldn't be human without it. Sorrow occurs through difficulty, but it is also what makes us understand joy. Professor and best-selling author Brene Brown says, "Owning our sadness is courageous and a necessary step in finding our way back to ourselves and each other."[5] Art can put sorrow on view for a means of connection with others who are empathetic

---

5. Brené Brown, *Atlas of the Heart* (New York: Random House, 2021), 106.

to suffering. Art that expresses sorrow is an attempt to reach others with similar experiences or like minds.

Balance

Art can be a balancing agent to help us access our multiple selves at any given time. Art can explore our various selves, the ones that are calm and contented, but also the ones that are anxious, confused, heartbroken, and afraid. Art can be an attempt to balance emotional states, handle stress, and navigate difficulty. It can also be used to demonstrate contentment, centeredness, and well-being. Or it can demonstrate the polarities of balance.

Self-Awareness

The poet Mark Nepo says, "I learned that when we write about ourselves deeply enough, we discover the world. And when we write about others deeply enough, we discover ourselves."[6] Inherent in his quote is the notion that one must explore deeply, the self and others, to gain awareness. Art can help the artist understand themselves and hold it up to the world as a demonstration and ownership of the essential self, their identity as they perceive it.

Extension of Experience

Everything we have experienced, from birth to right now, is the total of our understanding of the world we live in. It is the glass that makes our cultural lens. Art can extend to others the view through your eyes into your unique set of

---

6. Mark Nepo, *Drinking from the River of Light* (Louisville, CO: Sounds True, 2019), 107.

experiences. It is your worldview, the experience of what it is like to be you. It is an acknowledgment that your immense experience holds meaning within yourself and beyond.

Sensitivity

Art brings specifics and details to the forefront, often making the ordinary or the mundane noteworthy. Art can illuminate details, making others sensitive to their own world. It is concerned with the subtle, intuitive, or insightful, bringing comprehension into the viewer's experience.

These seven functions are not intended to be all inclusive. If you look at your work as a useful tool in the world, there are certainly more purposes for your tool. This is a guide to get you started in thinking about how your work functions in the world and for you.

HOW TO USE THE TOOLS TO UNDERSTAND PURPOSE

Look at the work you have made over the past year and think about it through these various functions described above. On a scale of 0–10, with 10 being the strongest use of this concept in your work, fill in the chart on the next page. I have included an "other" line if you discover something in your work that can't be assigned to these concepts. But before using "other," make sure you are thinking deeply about the functions presented and defined. As you think about your work through these definitions, ask yourself the questions on the next page. Then color in the number that coincides with the degree to which your work reflects the definition. See my example after the blank grid for further clarification.

Questions to Consider

- Memory: Does your art act to enhance memory, physical or sensory, and make those memories accessible to others?

- Hope: Does your art convey a sense of hope that transcends difficulties of life?

- Sorrow: Does your art put sorrow on view for a means of connection with others who are empathetic to suffering?

- Balance: Does your art attempt to balance emotional states, handle stress, navigate difficulty, and/or demonstrate contentment, centeredness, and well-being?

- Self-Awareness: Is your art a demonstration and ownership of the essential self, your identity as you perceive it?

- Extension of Experience: Does your art extend to others the view through your eyes into your unique set of experiences?

- Sensitivity: Does your art illuminate details, making others sensitive to their own world?

- Other: Is your art serving as a tool for another type of experience not listed here?

Here is the blank grid for you to fill in.

	0	1	2	3	4	5	6	7	8	9	10
Memory											
Hope											
Sorrow											
Balance											
Self-Awareness											
Experience											
Sensitivity											
Other (define											

Here is how I filled in my grid as I reflected on my recent work:

	0	1	2	3	4	5	6	7	8	9	10
Memory					▓						
Hope	▓										
Sorrow	▓									▓	
Balance									▓		
Self-Awareness											▓
Experience						▓					
Sensitivity											▓
Other (define											

HOW TO INTERPRET YOUR CHART

Your responses now become a way to understand your work. If your chart is very high in any one area (9 or 10), your work is probably extremely focused; you have likely been concentrating on your message and producing work in this consistent message. In the example, the chart demonstrates that I focus heavily on self-awareness and sensitivity.

But what if you are ready for a radical change? What if you feel it coming but don't know what you are looking for? Look at the areas where you rated the tool the lowest, least used concept in your work (0 or 1). If you want to make a dramatic shift in your work, concentrating on one of the low functions would give you the shake-up you need. For example, in my chart, the least important aspect is hope. It doesn't mean I don't care about it. It means I don't use it in my current body of work. So if I want to really challenge myself, to make a radical change, I need to consider how to integrate ideas or aspects of hopefulness.

If you don't seek a radical change, but are looking more toward a shift, look at the function that scored in the upper middle of the chart (6 or 7). This is an area you are already working in but could take further. Could you stress that function more, making it as important as the primary function? For example, my chart demonstrates that I'm using my work, to some degree, for emotional balance. I might ask myself, "What can I push in my work to more clearly integrate ideas of balance?"

The lower middle numbers (3, 4, and 5) are places where you think about these concepts but they haven't taken prominence. These are areas you've put some thought into, but these thoughts don't dominate your process. These, like the upper-middle numbers are places to consider more gentle shifts. In my example, this is memory. This is somewhat present in my work now, but if I want to shift my work, I could integrate memory in a way that is more evident.

What if your chart is a fairly consistent line? This means you are working across the functions without any taking prominence. If you want to shake up your work, pick a function that appeals to you—say for instance, memory. For the next several pieces, see if you can focus solely on memory, exploring the various meanings implied there. This means you are urging this function to move higher. When you do, something else will probably move lower.

The goal is not to have every tool equally present or be at a 10 on everything. That would probably make your work confusing to the viewer and very likely to you. In fact, there is no goal here. This is simply a way to think about how your work functions for you, what tools you employ as you make your work and convey your message.

If you use this chart to analyze your art's purpose, you might consider revisiting it as your work shifts, changes, and grows. Each new body of work may employ different tools depending on the messages you are conveying. For example, my chart looks very different when I am working on social commentary subjects than it looks in my recent work, which is very focused on studying the human interior.

This exercise can be most useful to help you:

· Understand your art and why you make it.
· Understand your role as a cultural voice for your generation.
· See avenues for shifting your voice and message, whether you seek a radical or a subtle shift.
· See places where your interests can speak to others through your work.

Notice the terminology above—enhance, change, suggest, attempt, demonstrate, acknowledge, comprehend—these are "tool" words. Words that change thoughts into actions. If your art does any of these things, this is a fine opportunity to view your work as a necessary tool that has a message important to your community and culture.

CHAPTER 2:
WHAT YOU BELIEVE ABOUT ART

Just about every artist I know has some degree of difficulty translating the message of their art into words. Yet artists are constantly asked to speak and write about their work. In gallery talks, we are trying to engage our audiences by sharing something about the work without interrupting the viewer's first-hand experience of it. In artist statements, we are trying to use a few brief sentences to open the door to our complex work, sometimes with a limited number of characters in which to express our deep and complicated urges, images, and processes. In chance encounters, we are asked, "What do you do?" and have to make a split-second decision about how to sum up the depths of our work in a brief and casual yet meaningful exchange. Doing the homework so that you express yourself well in these situations is key to making these experiences more valuable, useful, and even enjoyable.

Neil Gaiman's book *Art Matters* is a short but powerful manifesto of his intertwined life and art. He makes definitive statements on his beliefs, his truths. For example, he believes "It is difficult to kill an idea because ideas are invisible and contagious, and they move fast."[7] Some reasons I like this book are because it can be read in one sitting; has no extraneous words or long descriptions; is hand-written and illustrated (by Chris Riddell), so it feels personal, like an artist's sketchbook; and includes first-person, real-life experiences depicting how and why Gaiman built a creative life.

This is not an advice book; it is Gaiman's manifesto, his declaration of what, through his own personal experiences, is true and reliable for him. And while it is interesting and offers some useful advice, it is not designed as a guidebook—his manifesto cannot be mine. We have different experiences and work in different creative fields. But it did encourage me to think about my own manifesto—my core beliefs about my work, life, creativity, and artistic place in the world. Here is how I found this book most useful: we can use Gaiman's format to think through our own core beliefs and translate those thoughts about our work into words about our work.

THE MANIFESTO FORMAT

The word *manifesto* comes from the similar Latin word meaning to "make public." It is a statement or declaration

---

7. Neil Gaiman, *Art Matters* (New York: William Morrow: 2018), 1–11.

of one's position or platform. In four very short chapters, Gaiman succinctly presents how he has shaped his creative life. Personal and introspective, that's what a manifesto is—unique to the author. In chapter 1, "Credo," he presents ten statements of belief about ideas. This is his overarching statement on inalienable thoughts about ideas, where they come from, who has access to them and how they should be used. In chapter 2, he discusses "Why Our Future Depends on Libraries, Reading and Daydreaming." Since he is a novelist, it makes sense that he would think deeply about how we access books, reading, and its importance to us as a culture. In chapter 3, "Making a Chair," Gaiman explains the process of putting his office chair together. While, on the surface, this doesn't seem like manifesto material, but he is actually talking about ritual—what creative people do to transition from outside-of-the-studio thinking into creative thinking. In chapter 4, "Make Good Art," Gaiman tells his creative history. But this chapter is really about his experience of living a creative life and how that translates into advice for us.

EXPLORING YOUR BELIEFS

Whether you realize it or not, if you are an artist, you already have a set of beliefs, some firmly held and some malleable. Since a manifesto is a statement of personal belief, we can't simply use Gaiman's method, but we can *adapt* his method. Here is my guide, adapted from his format, for thinking about and writing your own manifesto.

· Think about your core beliefs about art. Not *your* art, but art in general. What is art's purpose to you and to the world?

- Think deeply about art in our culture, how it is made, how it is shared, its value to our past and future. Then go a step further: what is *your* work's value to our culture? How does your work fit in the continuum of the history of art?
- Think about your art rituals, what you do to prepare to make the work, and what you do while making the work. What do you do after you make the work? Are there patterns that have become your artistic rituals? What do these rituals serve to accomplish?
- Think about your personal art history. What is your artistic path? Where did it originate? Who helped you along? Who, if anyone, hindered your progress and why? Why did you make the choices you made about processes, materials, and content? What did you learn from these choices? Where are you on your journey right now? If asked, how would you advise others based on your own creative path and experience?

After all this thinking, put your thoughts into words. I recommend using the creative space and materials of your art. Use paper, pencil, or pen, your direct handwriting, and illustrations if you wish. Or use a computer. After all, it is an art tool too.

THE MANIFESTO BENEFIT

Let's think even further, why should we do the hard work of finding words for our beliefs about our work? The manifesto will help you put your intentions, views, and purposes for art-making into words.

For more experienced artists, you'll quickly see how this exercise will benefit you in discussing or writing about your work. You'll have several avenues from which to choose—overarching beliefs, the functions of art, your process and materials, and what you've learned on your artistic path—any of which is great material for the short presentation, the long conversation, gallery talk, or grant application.

For emerging artists, this is the kind of thinking and talking about art that you'll encounter in workshops, critiques, classes, and degree programs, where you are asked to explore your work conceptually. As you think through and write about these points, you'll begin to see your manifesto evolve as your work focuses and matures.

THIS IS YOUR STUDIO WORK

I am a big advocate of the written word. We forget. We need reminders, even of our own thoughts and ideas, especially as we age. Start your manifesto by breaking it down into manageable bits. Address one bit a day for ten minutes. Think for five minutes and write for five minutes. Then go to your studio and post it on the wall where you can see it and be reminded of it as you work.

This is a rigorous thinking and writing exercise. You'll find that your ideas shift, change, and grow as you move into deeper territory and over time. Find a pace that is manageable for you. Once a week? Twice a week? A daily practice?

Here is a bit-by-bit approach with thinking and writing prompts.

Crafting Your Belief Statements

· Entry 1: In an "I believe" statement, what is art's purpose to you?

- Entry 2: In an "I believe" statement, what is art's purpose in the world?
- Entry 3: In an "I believe" statement, how has art's purpose changed over time?
- Entry 4: In an "I believe" statement, how has art functioned in your life?
- Entry 5: In an "I believe" statement, what are your rights and responsibilities as an artist?

How You View Your Art in Our Culture

- Entry 6: Why is viewing art important?
- Entry 7: Where does viewing art happen?
- Entry 8: What are the positives and negatives of where we encounter art?
- Entry 9: How has the importance and uses of art changed over time?
- Entry 10: What role does art play in our future?

Understanding Your Creative Ritual

- Entry 11: What do you do to transition from outside-of-the-studio thinking into creative thinking?
- Entry 12: What do you do to stay in creative thinking for long periods of time?
- Entry 13: What do you do to transition from creative thinking into outside-of-the-studio thinking?
- Entry 14: Are there patterns in your process that have become creative rituals?
- Entry 15: Are there rituals you can adopt to trigger the transition to creative thinking, like meditation, a 10-minute painting or drawing exercise, or turning on your salt lamp?

Your Personal Art History

- Entry 16: Who were your best and worst teachers, and what did they teach you?
- Entry 17: Who gave you the best bit of advice, what was it, and did you follow it?
- Entry 18: What was the path you took, the choices you made to learn about art?
- Entry 19: What were the advantages and drawbacks to the path of your artistic learning?
- Entry 20: What is the best advice you have for an emerging artist?

This is not something extra that you do in addition to your studio work—this IS your studio work. As an artist, it is your responsibility to understand your work so that you can effectively share it with the world.

CHAPTER 3:
SETTING INTENTIONS

Setting an intention and holding it at the forefront of our thought process helps focus the work and makes more clear the meaning behind the work. It creates a consistency that makes for cohesive exhibitions and clear voice. Choreographer and writer Andrew Simonet sums it up this way: "Planning is a skill we artists already have. We use it all the time in our practice. We imagine a thing that doesn't exist. We make a plan to bring it into existence. We implement that plan, responding to changes and discoveries. We deliver the finished work."[8] He uses the word *plan*; I use *intention*. Intentions can be very specific—"I will make art about the #metoo movement. Everything I do will contribute to this idea." To know with conviction what you want your work to communicate to the world is exciting and

8. Andrew Simonet, *Making Your Life as an Artist Workbook* (Artist U: Philadelphia, 2024), 9.

purposeful. But that isn't always how art processes operate. Sometimes we just don't know what our work is about. As Simonet said, we respond to changes and discoveries. Can intentions be vague? Of course! Vague intentions move into the exploratory—"I will create a series of pieces that explore shape," or "I will create a series of pieces only using pencils and ink," or "I will explore interpersonal relationships using fruit as the subject."

Whether specific, vague, or exploratory, it is good discipline and studio practice to set intentions, to hold in your mind the path you are on, even if you move on and off the trail or it becomes vague and difficult to see.

Think about it as travel. If you are planning a trip to Italy, you want to make room for wonderful, unplanned experiences to happen. But if you don't go with a plan, you could end up lost and confused and miss everything. Experienced travelers know to plan ahead but also how to stay aware of opportunities along the way. Studio intentions are the same. Set an intention, but leave open the possibility for the unexpected to occur, and then recognize it when that happens.

HOW TO DETERMINE WHERE YOU ARE NOW

You are likely working under a set of intentions whether you realize it or not. Looking at the big concepts and also the details of your work can point to your current intentions, which can lead you to setting a longer-term goal, broader intentions, for building a body of work.

Go into the studio today with the intention to look at the BIG PICTURE.

Look at your last four to six pieces; what do they all have in common? Are they pointing toward an overall idea or philosophical viewpoint? If so, this is your *big picture;* the overall-in-one-sentence what your current work is about. Write it down, post it on your studio wall and refer to it frequently, keeping your mind focused on your *big picture* ideas.

While simultaneously ...

Go into the studio today with the intention to look at the LITTLE PICTURE.

Look at the details of your work. How do the details relate to the big picture concepts you determined? How do the details work together to create an overall idea, mood, or sensory experience? If you look at those same four to six pieces, do the details feed your *big picture* message? Can you put into words how the details create the impression you are striving for? Write it down, post it on your studio wall, and refer to it frequently, keeping your mind focused on your *little picture* ideas.

But what if your *little picture* details are not feeding your message? Rethink the details. Do you need all of them? Or do you need different kinds of details that support your message better? Are these areas you can edit, pare down, eliminate, or change?

What happens if you see little to no consistency in your last four to six pieces? This points to focus. Perhaps you are still exploring materials and subjects and haven't found a consistency of concept. If so, keep working and repeat this exercise after you've made another four to six pieces, and until you find a common denominator. Keep revisiting this growing body of work until you see consistency, whether in a recurring element, principle, subject, or idea.

THE LITTLE/BIG SHIFT: WHAT IS HAPPENING?

You have two alternating perspectives to consider as you make your work. When you are in the intuitive active painting mode, you are seeing details; you are in *little picture* mode. When you step back, you are seeing the whole image, shifting to *big picture* concepts. Make it a point to spend time in *both* places, referring to the notes you posted on your studio wall. Yes, this is a brain shift. Yes, this keeps your eye on the overall message *and* the details that create that message. Yes, this is exhausting. Rest.

This is the challenge: finding your consistent message and understanding why you are creating this work.

This is the goal: understanding how every intuitive *and* thoughtful decision you make in your work contributes to your consistent message.

Ultimately, this deep understanding of the little and big picture of your work will point you toward a unified, cohesive idea, the underlying intention, making it easier to understand your work and how to talk or write about it.

CHAPTER 4:
UNDERSTANDING AND RECOGNIZING SATISFACTION

The song "Satisfaction" by the Rolling Stones has the word "no" in it thirty times. It has the word "try" in it thirteen times. These lyrics, and the score itself, are the ultimate anthem of frustration. We all share the experience from the song—"'Cause I try, and I try, and I try, and I try"—while in our studios searching for something we can't even name.

When Harry Potter returns to Hogwarts in book 7, *Harry Potter and the Deathly Hallows*, he enlists his friends to help him find an object. He's not sure what it looks like, has no clue where it is, and has limited time in a vast magical castle in which to explore.[9] This is what it feels like to be on the enigmatic path to satisfaction, and even fulfillment, in our

---

9. J.K. Rowling, *Harry Potter and the Deathly Hallows* (London: Bloomsbury Publishing, 2007), 594–595.

work. We aren't sure what we are looking for, we don't know how to find it, and we often feel pressure, whether self-imposed or not.

Artist Hannelore Baron (1926–1987) gives us a key to understanding satisfaction. She said, "There was a long time when I wasn't completely satisfied with what I was doing … not that I didn't think each collage was good, but they didn't have the message … finally when I felt I had the message, then I thought, okay, now."[10] Baron wasn't "completely" satisfied; each collage was merely "good," but when she found the "message," she moved from satisfaction to fulfillment with the simple acknowledgment—"okay, now." Her sense of serenity is palpable in this quote; you can almost feel her settling into herself and her profound awareness of her most effective and pleasing work to date.

Implicit in Baron's quote, Rowling's book, and the Rolling Stones' song are several useful messages:

- *Stay on a path of exploration; try and try and try and try.* Walking a path doesn't mean you are always in motion. Sometimes you walk; sometimes you rest so that you can walk again later. If you aren't tired, stay in the studio and keep trying. But stepping away and taking a break is necessary, especially if you are tired and/or frustrated. You risk making irrational decisions and undoing the good work that is there, whether you can see it or not. But you can't find your way if you aren't actively making. Rest and then return to your work and keep exploring.

---

10. Ingrid Schaffner and Mark Baron, *Hannelore Baron: Works from 1969-1987* (Washington, DC: Smithsonian Institution Traveling Exhibition Services, 2001), 10.

- *Recognize when the work is good.* All the trying in the world will not turn into art unless you train yourself to recognize when the work is good. Not perfect, good. Every square inch doesn't have to be wonderful for there to be moments of good. Each artist has their own feeling, their own way of knowing when the work is connecting. Recognize when it is good and hold on to that feeling. And remember: perfection is a goal and is, in fact, a form of self-censorship. Personally, I would rather my work be good and well-crafted than perfect, since perfection isn't attainable anyway.

- *Be grateful when the work is great.* Florida artists Martha Mahoney and Antoinette Slick describe the feeling of knowing when a piece is great in entirely different ways. Mahoney describes the urge to hold on to the piece, to sit with it, to keep it close. She says, "I find I'm mesmerized by it. I'm stunned by it. I can't part with it. It's mine. I can't wait to wake up and look at it again."[11] Slick has an entirely different experience. She describes the work drawing her in to further question it. For her, the painting is great when it continues to ask questions. She says, "For me, the word is 'why'? Why that color, why that shape, why repeat that symbol, why continue to ask why about that particular painting?"[12] Her great paintings engage her in an inquiry long after they are complete.

These illustrations attest to the unique, personal experience of knowing your work, of having the artistic maturity to understand that every piece isn't going to be

---

11. Martha Mahoney, personal interview, April 2, 2020.
12. Antoinette Slick, personal interview April 2, 2020.

great, but also knowing that when you get a great one, you will recognize it and be grateful in your own way. When the feelings of good work turn into the feelings of great work, you'll just know. Like Hannelore Baron, you'll think, "Okay, now."

WHAT DOES SATISFIED FEEL LIKE?

Satisfaction comes from the Latin concept of "to do enough." Not too much or too little, but enough. How do you know when enough is enough? If you are alone in your studio, what does satisfaction feel like?

You can't recognize satisfaction unless you are working. Without question, setting a routine for work time and break time is the best way to find a rhythm to your work and life. Work for a set amount of time; separate from it for a set amount of time. Repeat until you have established a routine. You'll be amazed at how much progress you'll make, how much art you will make. And you must have a developing body of work to understand and recognize satisfaction.

RECOGNIZE WHEN THE WORK IS GOING WELL. HOW?

Next time you are in your studio and the work feels good, notice that in your body. Take a moment to write down, to actually commit to paper how it feels when the work is going well. Post that on your studio wall. Add to that as you continue your studio practice. When you've created a list of what it feels like to make good work, write in big letters above that list—MY WORK IS GOING WELL WHEN THIS HAPPENS. Read this list every time you work in your studio. Eventually, you'll train yourself to recognize when the work is satisfying.

Here is what my list looks like.

The Work is Going Well When:

- I realize I am singing or dancing
- The collage fragments aren't talking to me; they are talking to each other
- I am aware of the hum of the sewing machine, a pleasant meditative sound
- My whole body is aware; all senses engaged
- I have no sensation of time
- My face is relaxed

BE GRATEFUL WHEN THE WORK IS GREAT. HOW?

Pray to gods, muses, spirits, nature, self. Thank the divine, for when the work is great; it is a universal gift to the world and not exactly yours anymore. These are pieces that are not only your teachers but also world teachers. Show it broadly, talk about it openly, but keep the work when you can because these pieces are pivotal to your understanding of your own work. These pieces are simultaneously personal and universal. When you can't keep the original work, keep excellent images and records of them, so when you need them again—remember they are your teachers—you know where to find them. Plus, one day you'll need these signpost pieces for your publications and your retrospective.

CHAPTER 5:
MATERIALS ARE MAGIC

The fact is that no matter what materials you use, no matter how much your best artist friend loves a certain brand of paint or brush, the tool and the material will act differently for you than for her. So much of what we know about materials comes from the direct experience of using them and shaping them to our needs. But this discussion isn't about *using* materials. If you want to learn how to use materials and tools, put down this book and go to your studio and use them. Practice leads to proficiency. But first, learn how to safely handle and dispose of materials.[13] Also, see chapter 8, "The Value of Community," for a discussion on workshops.

This discussion is about *understanding* your materials. Experienced artists know that certain art materials and tools

---

13. The US Consumer Protection Safety Commission requires art materials to have cautionary labeling. See cpsc.gov for more information.

are enchanted; they have transcended functionality and have moved into the realm of totem, talisman, or charm. They know with certainty that this particular tool or that specific color of paint has a remarkable influence on the positive outcome of their actions and decisions around art making.

I'm talking about magic. Yes, real magic.

In 2012, I was the Chaco Canyon National Historical Park Artist-in-Residence. My work is a combination of drawing, painting, and sewing, so I packed up my sewing machine and all my other materials and flew out for my month at the canyon. On the return trip, the airline damaged my sewing machine. When I took it to the repair shop, the guy said it was totaled. Like a car. To my great surprise, tears suddenly welled up in my eyes as I asked questions and refused to believe the machine couldn't be repaired. I'm certain the repair guy has never had a customer cry over their sewing machine. I went home with my newly purchased machine, not excited about learning a new tool, and still mourning my wrecked one. What is most compelling, though, was my emotional reaction. Why was the irreparable damage to my sewing machine such an emotional experience? The answer was clear: my sewing machine had been with me since graduate school. We had made a lot of art together during the previous twenty-plus years. We made failed and successful experiments; we made deeply personal images. In short, together, we made pieces that built my artistic career. I was the thinker, and it was the doer, the object that made my thoughts and visions come to life. Losing it so suddenly was shocking, and it took time to develop that kind of relationship with my new machine. This object, this tool, had transcended functionality and had become a talisman, an object with remarkable influence on my creative self. Poet Mark Nepo says, "When finally accepting that we relate to material rather than manipulate it, we discover what we create and are changed by the discovery."[14] I was changed by the understanding that my sewing machine was more than a tool; it was my creative partner.

Greenville, SC, artist Melinda Hoffman has a magic brush. She openly and freely talks about the brush using that term: "Calling it a magic brush is tongue in cheek, but also deadly serious." The original magic brush was given to her by her brother. She used it off and on for years. Over time, she realized the brush could "do anything." It could make thin lines and thick lines. It felt right in her hand, bulky enough to have weight and presence. The bristles had the right "flick."

"People say you are silly"—when she talks about the brush in magical terms—"I'm not being silly. I'm telling you about the emotional response to finding my magic brush. Remember in the *Wizard of Oz* where the witch says you've always had the power? That's what the brush is about," says Hoffman.[15]

There are many of these brushes in the world. It has only become one-of-a-kind because it is Melinda's brush and she understands the connection, the interdependence between that tool and her creative self.

HOW ART SUPPLIES BECOME ENCHANTED

Artist Sophie Taeuber-Arp dedicated her career to the intersection of design and material, not only how to use

14. Nepo, *Drinking from the River of Light*, 37.
15. Melinda Hoffman, personal interview, 2020.

them well and for her purpose, but also what the materials mean, how they have symbolic significance. Her wise words—"Try to comprehend the nature of the material"—is a short sentence with a powerful message.[16] Give your studio tools and materials some serious thought. Look through your collection. Is there a certain canvas, paper, ink, stamp, marker, pen, hammer, X-Acto knife, thread, color, etc., that you go to when you need help? Is there a color that you know always helps you resolve problems? Is there a pen that makes just the right mark when you need it? Make a list of the *really* special tools and materials. And then go a step further—why are they special? Try to "comprehend their nature" as Taeuber-Arp said. They became enchanted somehow. Examine that.

For example, here is my list:

Magic Material or Tool	Why is it magic?
X-Acto knife that I used in my very first design job	This simple tool brings back memories of my first design job as a twenty-year-old. I was an important member of a creative team, and this tool reminds me of that start.
Bernina sewing machine	I am with it constantly, every time I work. It is an enduring presence on my worktable. It has its own space, its own sounds, its own needs. It does everything I ask it to.
Sulky thread	This thread is shimmery and silk-like without the expense of silk. It reflects light in a way that almost glows. And it is very strong. I ask a lot of my thread, and it responds.
Uniball Signo white paint pen	It writes on everything without fail and is bright, crisp, heavily pigmented, white paint in a pen that's easy to hold and use.

---

16. Medea Hoch and Bettina Kaufmann, *Sophie Taeuber-Arp* (London: Tate Publishing, 2021), 6.

Now, make your list.

Magic Material or Tool	Why is it magic?

PARTNERING WITH YOUR MATERIALS

Your materials and tools help shape your artistic identity, the way you think of yourself as an artist. Isn't that vitally important? And the by-product of your magic materials and tools is present and visible in the finished work. They are the elves in the studio, always there waiting for the next session with you, always supporting you and contributing to your work.

To be an artist, you need them.

For art to exist, they need you.

This seems an important reason to acknowledge the magic that emerges when you partner with something as simple as a special tube of alizarin crimson, or a perfectly crafted sable hair brush, or a pair of scissors that feels just right in your hand.

CHAPTER 6:
FINDING FOCUS

In order to understand what *focus* means, a quick Google search with the terms "quotes" and "focus" will turn up hundreds, if not thousands of hits. Many of these are from professional athletes who have spent their lives focusing. Olympian and World Cup soccer champion Abby Wambach said, "I know I was put on this planet to be an athlete."[17] She spent her childhood and young adult life proving that focus was the way to achievement.

Athletes understand the value of such intensity to improve their skills, their mental connection, and their ambition. Keep in mind that these are professional athletes; many have been practicing their crafts since they were children. And throughout their formative years, they have played with and against high-quality teammates and opponents. They've

---

17. "Abby Wambach Quotes," BrainyQuote.com, accessed March 19, 2024, https://www.brainyquote.com/quotes/abby_wambach_700969.

been through experimental phases and found what they are good at. As seasoned professionals, they have moved through their apprenticeships, found the skills they excel in, then honed their unique crafts.

This is a nearly perfect analogy for the artist. It is impossible to focus your work when you are a beginner, nor should you try. You don't know what you are good at until you've experimented. A beginner should be on an exploration of materials, concepts, and processes. Like athletes, eventually, the beginner advances to skillful, learning what drives their interests. This is where focus begins.

If you are a newcomer to art-making, experiment with lots of different materials, techniques, and subjects. Take workshops from a variety of teachers who teach a variety of processes. (For more information see chapter 8.) This is a great way to learn what you like, how materials will react under your hands, and what subjects compel you. When you've been around a while, when you've started exhibiting and sharing your work on social media, when you are toying with the idea of gallery representation and showing your work on a broader scale, I have some serious advice for you. Find focus.

WHAT DOES FOCUS MEAN?

Let's look at an album, a collection of music held together by a binding concept, as an example of focus. Rapper Eminem said, "The album requires a certain focus of mine that I can't really explain—let's just say it's all I can really do while I'm doing it."[18] He can't really explain the focus because focus isn't about *knowing* what you are going to do. Focus is about *stating the essential questions* you want to explore, having built the confidence and the skill to explore those questions, and putting your attention to *discovery* around those questions, without distraction of new processes, materials, and ideas. Eminem is compelled (making an irreversible decision) to explore his essential question. It is all he can do. This is what makes his albums cohesive.

REASONS TO FOCUS

Writer Peter London clearly articulates the personal and universal result of focusing your work. He said, "When we are motivated to find increasingly complete and satisfying means to convey what is of great personal importance, and draw from both the conscious and subconscious levels, our images naturally become more vivid, deeper, more articulate, and (interestingly!) somehow more universal."[19] He is talking about how focus has outward and inward benefits.

Outward

When you approach galleries, they want to see that your work is cohesive. When they sell your work, they want to know that you can produce on that level again, that the next piece you bring is going to be consistent with

---

18. Jonathan Cohen, "Exclusive: Eminem Talks New Album, Book," *Billboard*, posted December 12, 2008, https://www.billboard.com/music/music-news/exclusive-eminem-talks-new-album-book-266116/.

19. Peter London, *No More Secondhand Art* (Boston: Shambhala, 1989), 21.

what they are already promoting in your work. When you approach a museum, the curator wants to know that the work is professional, well crafted, and has something to say to their audience. Museums have an educational mission; the work must further their mission. Liz Miller, curator at the Myrtle Beach Art Museum says, "Consistency is my museum staff's motto. Consistency of message and writing style for all exhibition-related materials (i.e., artist statement, bio, verbiage about individual works, etc.) is of the utmost importance. If an exhibition of work is strong, but the consistency of message is not there, I'll typically hold off from booking it, keeping it on the back burner until I see that, over time, the art and its thematic content have evolved into a clear, succinct body of work."[20]

Miller describes working with an emerging artist who showed great potential for museum exhibition, but his work was unfocused, and he was confused about his message. After their conversation in his studio, he refocused his work and, months later, had a strong body of work and a very successful museum show. "That special exhibit was one that many of our visitors still talk about to this day," says Liz. When the artist focused, his message became more in line with the museum's mission, resulting in success for both.

Inward

In his excellent book on creativity, musician, producer, author, Questlove says, "If a question comes into perfect focus, answering it isn't a creative act anymore. It's more

---

20. Liz Miller, personal interview, 2022.

a matter of information retrieval." What he's saying here is that focus is fuzzy; it is an exploration around an idea, and it will not and should not be fully formed when you start. He goes on to say, "The second a question comes into view, the search process starts."[21] So your exploration around your question is your art making; you are creating focus as you mine your essential question.

Focus is a type of discipline. Focus asks, "Can you stick with this idea until you learn what you are looking for?" Focus asks, "Can you stay with this process until you've mastered it, until your craftsmanship is expert?" Focus says, "If you can stay with me, your work will get stronger, and you will know more about your work, yourself, and even your world as a result." And I ask you, "If your art is an exploration of yourself and your world, can you afford not to focus? Can you afford not to try and answer the compelling question?"

STEP BY STEP GUIDE TO FINDING FOCUS

Step One

Pull together two pieces from any period in your work. The first piece is one you nailed, one that you consider your best, most successful work. The second piece is one that you are happy with, satisfied. It is good.

Study these pieces side by side. For the first piece, the "best" one, write three things that are working about this piece. What did you do so well here that makes you have this feeling of accomplishment around it? For the second

---

21. Questlove, *Creative Quest* (New York: Ecco, 2018), 125.

piece, the one you are "satisfied" with, write three things that you could have done to make this piece better. Take these two lists to your studio, post them on the wall. They are now your focus guide, your set of rules. One is what you know you do well, the other is suggestions for what you can do to make the work better.

Step Two

When you have worked on a compelling idea in the past, how many pieces did you make before you became bored with it or felt the need to move on? If the answer is a low number, one to five, your work might tend to be scattered across processes and ideas. If your answer is higher, five to ten, you are starting to find value in staying with an idea, but you might not be fully aware of the potential benefits of focus. If your answer is over ten, you are focusing and might benefit from seeing just how far you can take a series.

The assignment: find your boredom point and add three to that. This is the target number of pieces for your next series. For example, if you abandon an idea after making four pieces about it, set your goal at seven. If you stay with an idea until you make ten pieces, see if you can stay with it until you make thirteen. Going beyond the boredom point will teach you how to stick with the idea, work through slumps, and take every piece to full completion—not just OK, but fully realized, strong work.

Step Three

Follow the rules. Your two lists—what you do really well and what you can do to improve your work—become your rules to follow. Start making the set number of pieces. You can make them one at a time, in pairs, or in sets, or you can bring them all up simultaneously. But reach by making at least three pieces more than you would beyond your boredom threshold.

What Not to Do

Do not add any new materials, ideas, or processes once you have set your rules. When embarking on a difficult challenge, start with what you know. Take on a difficult challenge by building on your current skill set. Bakers start with small cakes and pastries and move to the difficult tiered and layered cakes. Musicians start with a single instrument and move into complexity and composition. Start where you are now, with a strong understanding of what it is you do well (your lists/rules) and do it deeper and broader.

Don't break the rules. The rules you created from what you already do well are your best guide to confidence, problem-solving, and taking your work forward. The rules for what you could do better are helpers, pushing you to go just a bit further.

What to Expect

After about two to three pieces, you'll want to abandon the whole exercise. Don't do it. You made yourself a promise, and you need to stick to it for your art and for your confidence. John Daido Loori says, "Wait in the presence of the subject until your presence has been acknowledged and you feel that a bond has been created. … Subjects change with time. They reveal different aspects of themselves if you're able to be patient and allow this revelation to unfold."[22] You are learning a very valuable lesson in how to move through frustration and manage boredom by staying with the series. Look at your lists; there are clues there in moving toward resolution of a piece. Use what you did in your best work to point you toward what you can do when you are struggling.

After about five pieces, you'll think you were too ambitious. You'll think, "Who am I to think I could do twelve?" You can. Ted Lasso said, "Taking on a challenge is a lot like riding a horse, isn't it? If you're comfortable while you are doing it, you're probably doing it wrong."[23] Motivation and personal importance are keys to staying with a difficult project. Recall the enthusiasm of when you were just starting the series and use that as your spirit guide. Recognize that it might feel uncomfortable and just accept that and keep going forward.

At any point along this path, you'll question, and perhaps even be angry with me for talking you into this. That's OK; I can take it. As a college professor, I am very familiar with frustration with assignments. You may talk about me behind or in front of my back. And if you experience this, please read the following again and again:

> *This process works. I have tested it with many artists, and I have seen amazing growth in the craftsmanship of managing materials and in the*

---

22. John Daido Loori, *The Zen of Creativity* (New York: Ballantine Books, 2005), 89.

23. *Ted Lasso*, season 1, episode 1, "Pilot," directed by Tom Marshall, written by Jason Sudeikis, Bill Lawrence, and Brendan Hunt, aired on August 14, 2020, on Apple TV.

depth of the concepts around the work. Staying with an idea for a sustained period of time will take you into deeper learning about yourself and the work, it will take you to a deeper understanding of your materials and imagery, and, upon completion, it will take you to levels of satisfaction that you've never experienced before.

Florida artist Pat Zalisko attests to this process. When she first encountered this exercise, she set her goal at fourteen pieces and began to get bored around nine. With five left to go, she needed a way through the boredom without breaking the rules. She shifted the size of the canvas and the orientation as she entered into the last few pieces. That was enough to keep her interested. "One thing that you asked me to do was determine three qualities of my own strongest art. I wrote them down, and they are still posted on my studio wall. They serve as a constant reminder," she said of the process. Of the work, she said, "Regrets? None! I learned from the process. The body of work was successful with several pieces going into an exhibition at the Baker Museum's 'Florida Contemporary' exhibit in Naples, Florida."[24] Further, this cohesive body of work led to another exhibition and a solo show at a gallery.

The key to success in this exercise is tenacity and trust. Stick with it and don't stray. Find ways through your boredom so that you learn how to get over a rough patch

---

24. Pat Zalisko, personal interview, April 21, 2020.

without abandoning your idea. Trust that there are rewards found along the path and at the end.

Look back at Peter London's quote on page 45. His concepts are the building blocks and benefits of focus. Look at the key words in his quote:

- *Motivation*. to gain focus, you need to want it enough to stay with it.
- *Personal*: to gain focus, it must be meaningful to you on a deep level.
- *Conscious and subconscious*: to gain focus, you must acknowledge and access both the thinking and the intuitive parts of your brain.
- *Naturally*: to gain focus is a sort of magic into deeper levels of art-making. Allow the work to happen.

And London asserts, correctly in my opinion, that if the artist engages in these concepts, the work becomes richer, more meaningful, more personal, and more universal. The work resonates, and the artist grows.

CHAPTER 7:
THE INNER CRITIC

We often seek the advice of others through critiques, classes, and many other types of conversations with those we respect and admire. What do you do with their advice? Author Neil Gaiman offers a funny aside:

> "I started trying to think what the best advice I'd been given over the years was. And it came from Stephen King twenty years ago, at the height of the success of Sandman. … His advice was this: 'This is really great. You should enjoy it.' And I didn't. Best advice I got that I ignored. Instead I worried about it. I worried about the next deadline, the next idea, the next story. … I wish I'd enjoyed it more. I was too worried about things going wrong, about what came next, to enjoy the bit I was on. That was the hardest lesson for me I think: to let go and

enjoy the ride, because the ride takes you to some
remarkable and unexpected places." [25]

Besides being a powerful reminder to stay present and recognize your own small and large moments of greatness, in this quote, Gaiman admits to getting superb advice from someone he respects and admires, and still, he doesn't take the very good advice he gets. Why? The inner critic is sitting on his shoulder telling him to worry. So the discussion here is not about whether to take advice; it is about the role of the inner critic.

ENEMY OF ART OR TRUSTED FRIEND?

To be clear, it isn't a bad thing to have an inner critic. The inner critic helps us to stand back and look objectively at our work, to attempt to see our work from the viewer's perspective and to make our work have relevance and meaning to others. All of this is good and necessary.

But it is impossible to be creative when the inner critic is constantly sitting on your shoulder asking questions. *Why that color? Why this shape? Why that symbol?* Your brain is trying to work from a spontaneous and intuitive space while simultaneously trying to process why you are making each decision and if it is the correct one. This is too much movement between brain processes. Ultimately, we become tired, frustrated, and discouraged and enter into profound self-doubt. *Why am I doing this? How can I call myself an artist? This work is awful.* It won't be long before quitting

---

25. Gaiman, *Art Matters.*

enters the picture, and then the world is deprived of your creative expression, your artistic historical mark, and the inner critic has become the enemy of your art instead of providing you the service of objectivity.

A NOTE ON PERFECTION

Many artists have trouble with striving for perfection. Perfection is not only impossible, but also a form of self-censorship. It is a signal that you are overly critical of your work and can't recognize when something great might be happening. You miss it. This means that in your pursuit of perfection, you are actually creating a barrier to your own creativity. It causes artists to withhold their work from view, to work pieces to death, to cause the art to lose freshness and energy. Perfection is not frustration. In fact, frustration can be a powerful creative tool. Perfection is self-defeating and consuming. It will paralyze creativity. The goal is not for the work to be perfect; the goal is for the work to get made and be seen. The inner critic can actually help with that.

PEOPLE, DON'T FIGHT WITH YOUR ART

The word *critic* comes from the Greek *kritikos*, which means to judge. The word *intuit* comes from the Latin word meaning to contemplate. Judging and contemplating are two distinctly different actions. Sound judgment can only occur once contemplation has happened. We see this in every facet of our public and private lives—school, court, friendships, partnerships, and marriages. Thoughtful contemplation precedes sound judgment. Why, then, do artists let the critic sit on our shoulders *while* we work, *while* we are striving to stay in our intuitive mode? Why do we try to work and judge simultaneously? Many of you know from personal experience what this does to you—it leads to discord with yourself and your art.

It is only logical that the making of art and the critiquing of art should be separate but equally important activities with the artist and the inner critic mutually respecting one another. But how do we separate them?

CHANGE YOUR MIND

Think of the inner critic as an advisor, a trusted friend, always there when you need them and to lend advice when you seek it. Like any good advisor or trusted friend, the inner critic needs to stay out of your studio until invited in at the appropriate time. You wouldn't have your best friend watch and judge you while you work. Why would you let the inner critic do that?

Then, when you are ready to take a step back and evaluate, it is time to invite the critic back in. Remember that the inner critic has an important and necessary job to do. And when invited in, the inner critic should be kind, honest, and respectful of the space, the work there, and most of all, the artist. You must treat *you, the artist,* and *you, the inner critic,* as you would a trusted friend and advisor, with kindness and courtesy.

EMBRACING THE INNER CRITIC

Most artists have some prep or set up time before they shift into creating. Allow the inner critic, your trusted friend, to be with you during this set up time. Let the inner critic ask questions, make suggestions, as if there was an actual trusted friend in your studio with you. Then, when you are ready to start, open the door, tell the critic to take a walk, and close the door behind them. This sounds ridiculous, but it is the act of thinking about the inner critic as someone other than you and as someone you trust, and telling them, like everyone else, *"You are not welcome here while I am working."* Some artists find setting a time limit useful; some would rather work until they are ready for a break. However you do this, do not allow the critical voice in your head while you are in your creative space. You have politely asked the critical voice to leave for a while. Now let it.

When time is up, open the door and invite the critic back in, shifting your mind from the creative to the critical space. Then have a reasonable conversation with yourself about what you just made. Don't say anything to yourself that you wouldn't say to another artist. Like you would with an artist friend, enter into critical and honest, but polite, discourse about your work with yourself. A good critic wouldn't tell an artist their work is awful. A good critic would search for the successful and unsuccessful in the work and carefully put that message into words.

This is a process of moving in and out of your creative and critical head spaces. Successful artists know they need both. They need freedom to make the work uninhibited by comment, suggestion, or judgment from anything outside of the creative space. They also know they need to step back from the work and see the big picture (see chapter 3, "Setting Intentions"). They need to objectively view their work to move the composition and the message forward. And most importantly, they need to be able to do this alone, in their own studios, without anyone else's help or influence.

CHAPTER 8:
THE VALUE OF COMMUNITY

Artists spend a lot of time alone in their studios. We need this; we choose it. But just like professionals in other fields, artists need feedback. Scientists, mathematicians, and historians all go to conferences to refresh, renew, and rethink. In fact, many words that begin with *re-* are the reasons we seek community and companionship within any given discipline:

- *Retreat:* to rest and contemplate in a secluded place
- *Revise:* to amend in order to correct, update, or improve
- *Respond:* to act or do something in reaction to something else
- *React:* to respond to something by showing the feelings or thoughts it arouses
- *Recommend:* to suggest something as worthy of being accepted, used, or done

- *Refresh:* to prompt or reactivate the memory with a piece of information
- *Remember:* to keep in mind for attention or consideration
- *Recognize:* to accept the validity or truth of something
- *Realize:* to know, understand, and accept something
- *Represent:* to symbolize or stand for something; to portray or present one thing as another
- *Return:* to go back to something already considered to deal with it more thoroughly or conclusively
- *Remind:* to cause somebody to remember or think of something
- *Review:* to consider, study, or check something again

WORKSHOPS, RETREATS and RESIDENCIES

Oh, the value of workshops, retreats, and residencies (WRR)! Here is where we stretch and grow in an environment of support and encouragement. This is where we test theories, practice using our voices, build communities and networks, forge artistic friendships, and learn about materials and techniques. There are so many valuable reasons to do this, so many ways to stretch and grow, and so, so, so many workshops, retreats, and residencies to choose from.

If you've never done WRRs, consider the value of having the experiences of quiet contemplation, developing your work, exercising your voice in giving feedback to others, realizing your own artistic worth, value, and voice, and building a network of like-minded artists. These are but a few of the direct benefits of joining others and studying as a community.

If you are a frequent WRR participant, compare the *re*-word list to your WRR memories and notes. Some, if not many, of these concepts should show up. Your experiences should include real learning that you took back to your studio and grew into over time.

WHERE SHOULD I START?

Artists can engage in larger learning communities in so many ways. Understanding these types of experiences can be useful in determining what is right for you.

Workshops will have an instructor. They are often technique and materials driven; in other words, you are learning something specific such as printmaking or encaustics. They can range from several hours to several days. Look at the instructor's experience in the material or technique being taught. Look at their work. Study with instructors whose work resonates with you.

Retreats will usually have a group leader who directs and monitors the experience and provides support and mentoring. Often, retreats will offer directed conversations and group critiques. They usually last several days to a couple of weeks and are held in a somewhat isolated community. Part of the point is to isolate to build group trust. Look at the retreat leader's resume for leadership experience. In addition to having their own exhibitions, have they judged shows, led critique groups, taught classes, written about art, or otherwise demonstrated leadership skills in the arts and creativity? A strong, experienced leader is an important element of a successful retreat.

Residencies will sometimes have a leader, but are most often a work-on-your-own experience. Many artists seek the residency experience because it allows them the space and time to immerse themselves fully in their work. This might be in a cloistered community with other creatives who are each working on their own. Most are competitive, requiring an application, description, and images of your work, and selection is made by a panel. There may be a community responsibility like presenting a talk, organizing and participating in a panel, or teaching. Residencies range in duration from several weeks to a couple of years. These are considered long range, career development experiences and often are considered noteworthy on a resume. Understandable, since the organization is investing their resources in that artist for a considerable time period.

If you are a newcomer to art, workshops can help you determine the techniques and materials you want to pursue. Take the techniques you learned back to your studio and practice. Become proficient in your voice and materials.

Once established in your materials and techniques, seek retreats to build your network, and work closely with an experienced professional interested in your development. Even a few days in the retreat environment is enough to find the supportive network that can help sustain you when you are alone in your studio.

If you are building a career in the arts, residencies can bring attention to your work and offer space, time, and exposure. They require a significant time commitment, so be sure this is something you want to do before you apply.

Remember, everything has a price, and the cost of WRRs vary dramatically. Read all of the information carefully so you know the financial commitment, housing, meals, and studio arrangements, and especially the refund and cancellation policy.

DECIDING ON THE BEST FIT

Every workshop I've attended, every retreat I've participated in, every residency for which I've been selected—all have been on the recommendation of artists I respect and admire. Fortunately, we have social networks that help us see what is available, but never underestimate the value of a personal, word-of-mouth recommendation.

If you are fairly well established, you have a network of artist friends. Ask them about their experiences. Who would they study with if they had a chance? Look at work. Whose work speaks to you, and do they offer workshops? Call colleges and university art departments. Speak with faculty in your discipline and see who they recommend. Contact me. I'll happily share with you the ones I have enjoyed and found artistically and creatively fulfilling. Most artists that I've encountered love sharing their experiences and will give you names and reviews.

BRINGING THE WRR EXPERIENCE INTO YOUR STUDIO

Remember that workshops and retreats are about growing, stretching, and experimenting. They aren't about demonstrating. If you are using your experience to grow, you will have mixed results—some satisfying work, some unsatisfying work. But remember, all of it is necessary for growth. At the end of a retreat or workshop, go home, unpack, and give yourself a few days to unwind. Not weeks or months—days! Then assess the work you did while it is still fresh in your recent experience. Think about your work on a scale of 1 to 5, where one is the least satisfying work and 5 the most satisfying. Here are some questions to consider.

For the work you consider 4 and 5, the most satisfying, acknowledge your satisfaction with this work, and take pride in your accomplishment. Give yourself this gift. Specifically, what worked? Put this into words; write it down. Are these pieces related in compositional elements or subject? Or both? If the pieces are related, here is a clue. Maybe there is a path here you could continue to explore, whether it is in subject matter or composition.

For the work you consider 1 and 2, the least satisfying, be kind to yourself as you look at this work. Don't say anything to yourself about this work that you wouldn't say to another artist. Give yourself this gift too. Look at the pieces through each compositional element. Can you determine specifically where the piece fell apart? Put this into words; write it down. Are there areas where the piece works? If so, what is working there, and can you apply that to the other areas of the piece? When you look at the successful work, is something there that you can apply to the least successful pieces to improve them? Above all, NEVER throw this work away immediately after the workshop. Even if it is very unsatisfying. It might have lessons to teach you later. Or it might become collage material or the base layer of later work.

It is useful to think about your WRR experience and even more useful to write down your thoughts. Translating your thoughts into words on paper sets down a record for your memory and also formulates language and vocabulary skills as they apply to the abstract thoughts around visual art.

Rarely do I find the workshop or retreat experience to be over when I leave the venue. It takes weeks and even months to process what happened there. So much interaction takes place—you and your work, critiques, conversations over coffee breaks, conversations over dinner. There are vivid moments from retreats that influence my studio practice, even twenty years later! Spend the time to debrief, to absorb the experience so that the important information about what was and wasn't successful will move fluidly into your studio practice.

CHAPTER 9:
ARTISTS WILL FIND A WAY

There is a difference between having an artistic practice and living a creative life. Living creatively means that the artist sees the creative process in every moment of life, including the studio, but also and, maybe even more importantly, in everything else, everyday. When I made this discovery, I saw that the topics of this book can apply to gardening, decorating, writing, reading, cooking, dancing, meditating, learning—everything we humans do in our daily lives for work and for pleasure. What we call "art" is a by-product of this kind of creative beingness.

Many years ago, an artist in one of my retreats asked a question I continue to consider. She said, "I get so much from your retreats, but what do you get?" The same could be asked about this book. What do I get? Or more specifically, what do I want?

I want to be with creative people. We are the believers. We know and understand that it isn't necessary to know and understand, but to recognize curiosity and then follow it, just to see where it goes, trusting that the path will unfold. Without judgment or expectation, but with pure delight and gratitude in the often difficult process and perhaps even the product. Questlove said, "How well you understand the original issue isn't the issue. It's how well it moves within your head. You're not being tested on your comprehension in a classroom setting. You're being asked to move out into the world and make something new."[26] It really is that simple.

But along the way, because we are artists, we think, we question, we analyze, we critique, we doubt. And because we are artists, we really want these answers. These questions are fundamental to creativity and vital to the artist's deepening. They are essential to living a creative life. They are how we get somewhere, how we make discoveries, how we get a glimpse of the divine in each of us, if we are willing to do the work.

This book is a pathway for discovering the answers to your deeply felt questions about your art. When you are alone in your studio questioning your creativity, your process, the meaning of your work, its place in the world, this book is your creativity assistant, holding your hand through the deeper questions of why you are an artist now, in a challenging world. Explore your artistic identity. Use your voice. Expand your knowing.

---

26. Questlove, *Creative Quest*, 186.

FURTHER READING

Brown, Brené. *Atlas of the Heart: Mapping Meaningful Connection and the Language of Human Experience.* New York: Random House, 2021.

De Botton, A., and J. Armstrong. *Art as Therapy.* London: Phaidon Press Limited, 2013.

Gaiman, Neil. *Art Matters: Because Your Imagination Can Change the World.* New York: William Morrow, 2018.

Gilbert, Elizabeth. *Big Magic: Creative Living Beyond Fear.* New York: Riverhead Books, 2015.

Godin, Seth. *The Practice: Shipping Creative Work.* New York: Portfolio, 2020.

Hoch, Medea, and Bettina Kaufmann. *Sophie Taeuber-Arp.* London: Tate Publishing, 2021.

London, Peter. *No More Secondhand Art: Awakening the Artist Within.* Boston: Shambhala Publications, 1989.

Loori, John Daido. *The Zen of Creativity: Cultivating Your Artistic Life.* New York: Ballantine Books, 2005.

Nepo, Mark. *Drinking from the River of Light: The Life of Expression.* Louisville, CO: Sounds True, 2019.

Questlove. *Creative Quest.* New York: Ecco, 2019.

Rubin, Rick. *The Creative Act: A Way of Being.* New York: Penguin Press, 2023.

Schaffner, Ingrid, and Mark Baron. *Hannelore Baron. Works from 1969 to 1987.* Washington, DC: Smithsonian Institution Traveling Exhibition Services, 2001.

Simonet, Andrew. *Making Your Life as an Artist Workbook.* Philadelphia: Artists U, 2024.

Wambach, Abby. *Wolfpack: How to Come Together, Unleash Our Power, and Change the Game.* New York: Celadon Books, 2019.

ACKNOWLEDGMENTS

This book, this work that I am so proud of, sat in my computer for years. I wrote most of it during the 2020 pandemic lockdown while I was on sabbatical. My first thanks must go to the University of South Carolina Lancaster for the valuable time to create. I have since retired and have been working with artists, talking with them about their work, helping them to excavate answers to the deeper questions about meaning, studying their work, writing essays that help promote their exhibits, and watching them grow and develop and take their work to the places they have chosen. And my book, the content very useful as I led retreats and workshops, sat more complete than I even realized, right there in my computer. I didn't know how to get it published. Then I met Tonya Reid at a party. Then she introduced me to her publishers, Cindy Urbanski and Shana Hartman. Then they introduced me to their designer, Melisa Graham. And in no time, there it was—completed. Not just the manuscript, but the fully formed, cover, pages, spine, nightstand-bookstack-ready book. Studio-ready book. How can I ever thank you, my publisher, colleagues, and friends?

Take a look through the Further Reading section for your required reading list. If I were your professor, these books would be on the syllabus. I recommend them at every retreat and workshop I lead. When an artist asks for help, these are the books that I refer them to. The authors of these books are my people. I have tried most sincerely to fully acknowledge them in the text, in the footnotes, and in the reading list. They propel us readers, artists, and creativity seekers to depths and breadth in how we think about our work. My deepest thanks goes to them for sharing work so that I can share mine.

For all of the artists who encouraged and have faith in this work, I thank you. There are a lot of you. Some new to working with me, some frequent fliers. You all make every part of my life as an artist and teacher richer. You know who you are. You are the ones who said, "Why don't you write a book?" So I did.

For my family and friends, thank you for believing that this was something I could do, something worthy to put into the world.

And for my husband, Van, who is his own kind of artist, thank you for ever believing in my powers, for ever encouraging me to do what I love.

ABOUT THE AUTHOR

Fran Gardner is Distinguished Professor Emerita of art and art history at the University of South Carolina Lancaster where she taught studio courses and art history for thirty-two years. Through these many years of teaching, she developed her methods for working with artists on their studio practices and creativity and gained the expertise for writing about art, leading retreats, teaching workshops, and judging and curating exhibitions. She works in mixed media collage with a heavy emphasis on fiber arts. She paints and draws with traditional materials, but also with thread, layering her work with rich texture, color and mark-making. Visit her online at frangardnerart.com or connect on Instagram @fran.gardner.

Made in the USA
Monee, IL
25 April 2024

57495230R00046